A TASTE OF CHICKEN SOUP

FOR THE

TEACHER'S SOUL

A TASTE OF CHICKEN SOUP

FOR THE

TEACHER'S SOUL

Stories to Open the Hearts and Rekindle the Spirits of Educators

Jack Canfield
Mark Victor Hansen

Health Communications, Inc.
Deerfield Beach, Florida

www.hcibooks.com
www.chickensoup.com

Why Choose Teaching? Reprinted by permission of Bonnie S. Block. ©1996 Bonnie S. Block.

Once a Teacher, Always . . . Reprinted by permission of Kay Conner Pliszka. ©2000 Kay Conner Pliszka.

Sarah. Reprinted by permission of Michele Wallace Campanelli. ©1999 Michele Wallace Campanelli.

Promises to Keep. Reprinted by permission of Kris Hamm Ross. ©1997 Kris Hamm Ross.

Standing by Mr. Donato. Reprinted by permission of Dennis McCarthy. ©1997 Dennis McCarthy. Appeared in The Daily News, April 9, 1997.

One of My Early Teaching Jobs. Reprinted by permission of Angela K. Nelson. ©1997 Angela K. Nelson.

Permission to Fail. Reprinted by permission of Tim Lindstrom. ©1991 Aletha Lindstrom.

So Little Meant So Much. Reprinted by permission of Beth Teolis. ©2000 Beth Teolis.

What I Learned in Spite of Myself. Reprinted by permission of MaryJanice Davidson Alongi. ©2001 MaryJanice Davidson Alongi.

You Never Picked Me Last. Reprinted by permission of Dr. Tee Carr. ©1997 Dr. Tee Carr.

Anna. Reprinted by permission of Isabel Bearman Bucher. ©1996 Isabel Bearman Bucher.

To Beth's First-Grade Teacher. Reprinted by permission of Richard F. Abrahamson. ©1984 Richard F. Abrahamson.

Library of Congress Cataloging-in-Publication Data is on file with the Library of Congress

©2006 Jack Canfield, Mark Victor Hansen
ISBN 0-75730-509-1

Publisher: Health Communications, Inc.
3201 S.W. 15th Street
Deerfield Beach, FL 33442-8190

We dedicate this book to those teachers everywhere who have committed their lives to educating, encouraging and empowering the students of our world.

Contents

Introduction

Having sat in the classrooms of many great teachers, having taught in the public schools, and having spent over twenty years training teachers, it is with great satisfaction and joy that we bring you this "taste" of our popular *Chicken Soup for the Soul* series.

Every day, along with a hundred million other parents, we entrust our children to you—the teachers. We appreciate your sacrifices, acknowledge your challenges and appreciate your contribution to our children. Faced with often overcrowded classrooms, ever-tightening budgets and increased expectations, you nevertheless continue to work your special magic with your students.

You have chosen the most challenging and most rewarding profession there is or ever will be. While it doesn't pay a lot in dollars, the psychological and emotional rewards are enormous—the light in the eyes of a newly motivated student; the smile on a face when a seemingly unfathomable concept is finally grasped; the delighted laughter of an estranged child who is finally included; the joy of watching a challenging student walk across the stage at graduation; the appreciative smiles, hugs and thank-yous from a grateful parent; a thank-you card from a potential dropout who decides to stay in school and goes on to succeed; and the internal satisfaction of knowing that you have made a difference, done something that matters and left an undeniable mark on the future.

Once again, please consider this book a giant thank-you card for all you have done for so many for so long.

Why Choose Teaching?

I touch the future. I teach.
CHRISTA MCAULIFFE

My family was gathered for a leisurely summer barbecue when the discussion arose about a celebrity who earned an excessive amount of money. I've forgotten if it was a sports figure or an actor. In today's society, it doesn't seem to matter. The major criteria for receiving mega dollars seem to be determined by how much the audience will pay to watch the performer achieve.

Then why choose teaching for a career? I only half-listened to their conversation as I pondered the answer to that question.

I remembered my three children watching me spend many nights and weekends planning for my class. I remembered how they intently listened to my frustrations concerning materials, procedures and the amount of responsibility that seemed to endlessly be thrust into the laps of classroom teachers. I remembered how they eagerly awaited to hear stories of my classroom children: those funny ones; those when the children had successfully achieved; and those when I shared my grave concerns about my students.

I remembered when it came time for each of my own children to choose a profession. How I waited to hear if any had plans to follow Mom into teaching. Long deliberations held no mention of anyone becoming a teacher. I sadly realized it was not even going to be a consideration. Their body language seemed to say, "Why would I choose teaching?"

Dessert was being served, and everyone was still engrossed in the discussion of the enormous salary of one individual, when the phone rang. My husband handed the phone to me, saying, "They're looking for Bonnie Block." Then he resumed eating his favorite dessert.

"Hello, this is Bonnie Block," I said, debating whether I should have even answered the phone during the family meal.

"Is this the Bonnie Block who used to teach kindergarten?"

A nervous sensation swelled in me, and my mind raced with memories of those days so long ago.

"Yes!" I exclaimed with a lump in my throat. It seemed like forever as I waited anxiously to hear what the caller would say next.

"I am Danielle—Danielle Russ. I was in your kindergarten class."

Tears of surprise and joy rolled down my flushed cheeks.

"Yes," I uttered softly as I remembered that darling, wonderful child.

"Well, I am graduating from high school this year, and I have been trying to find you. I wanted you to know what a difference you made in my life."

She proceeded to give details of how I made that difference. My influence on her wasn't limited to kindergarten but remained a strong motivating force when she needed a coach to help her meet a challenge. "I pictured you praising and encouraging me all the way."

Why choose teaching?

The pay is great!

Bonnie Block

Once a Teacher, Always . . .

Mom was a teacher most of her life. When she wasn't in the classroom, she was educating her children or grandchildren: correcting our grammar; starting us on collections of butterflies, flowers or rocks; or inspiring a discussion on her most recent "Book of the Month Club" topic. Mom made learning fun.

It was sad for my three brothers and me to see her ailing in her later years. At eighty-five, she suffered a stroke that paralyzed the entire right side of her body, and she went steadily downhill after that.

Two days before she died, my brothers and I met at her nursing home and took her for a short ride in a wheelchair. While we waited for the staff to lift her limp body back into bed, Mom fell asleep. Not wanting to wake her, we moved to the far end of the room and spoke softly.

After several minutes our conversation was interrupted by a muffled sound coming from across the room. We stopped talking and looked at Mom. Her eyes were closed, but she was clearly trying to communicate with us. We went to her side.

"Whrrr," she said weakly.

"Where?" I asked. "Mom, is there something you want?"

"Whrrr," she repeated a bit stronger. My brothers and I looked at each other and shook our heads sadly.

Mom opened her eyes, sighed, and with all the energy she could muster said, "Not was. Say were!"

It suddenly occurred to us that Mom was correcting brother Jim's last sentence, "If it was up to me . . . "

Jim leaned down and kissed her cheek. "Thanks, Mom," he whispered.

We smiled at each other and once again shook our heads—this time in awe of a remarkable teacher.

Kay Conner Pliszka

Sarah

*Sometimes the heart sees
what is invisible to the eye.*

H. JACKSON BROWN, JR.

I will never forget Sarah. In my eight years as a Head Start teacher, she was my most exceptional student.

One morning, the administrator had called my assistant and me into her office. She told us that we'd be getting a new student—a three-year-old named Sarah. "The girl has been abused," she said. Her father had poured a scalding bucket of hot water down her head, badly burning her neck, back, legs and scalp. She had no hair. Her back and legs would have to be wiped down with oil every few hours so they would not get stiff.

Sarah visited my preschool room the next day for an introductory meeting while the other students were out. Her facial features were petite, and she smiled up at me with innocent brown eyes, startlingly naked because her eyebrows were missing. The back of her bald head was badly scarred down to the neck. She wore a simple white sundress that showed her burnt arms. I seized with anger at her father. Then I worried about how the other children would react. I struggled to maintain calm in front of Sarah, her foster mother and my teaching assistant. After Sarah and her mom left, I gave into tears.

"We must prepare the students," my assistant reminded me. "We can't just let her walk in and be made fun of."

"To draw attention to her appearance would single her out," I said. After much discussion, we agreed to have Sarah come in for a half-day on her first day in order to ascertain how the children would react towards her.

The morning Sarah arrived she quietly took a seat. I watched her every second. During playtime, the other children talked to her and shared their toys. They didn't seem to notice she was different.

"It's dress-up time," one of my students reminded me. Every day before lunch, they all got to raid the closets and play in a collection of grown-up clothes and fanciful kid's costumes.

"Okay, everyone, let's get started," I agreed.

Sarah followed the other children and put on an Easter bonnet and princess outfit. I tried to smile, but the disparity between the delicate fabric and her scarred skin made me ache for her.

Sarah left after lunch. Here classmates had nap time, and then I led a vocabulary-building lesson.

Finally, I asked the children, "So how do you all like our new friend Sarah?"

One child answered. "Her hands are small."

Another added, "She picked the long skirt for dress-up."

Not one mentioned her thick skin or her missing hair.

The children's observations helped me realize something very valuable. We teachers saw Sarah as a child who had suffered greatly, a child who needed exceptional handling and assistance. We wanted to hold her, prove to her that not all adults were bad. The children, many of whom had also suffered in some way, saw beyond her scarred appearance. They saw another child, a peer, a new friend.

The next school day, during dress-up, Sarah put on the princess clothes again.

She stood in front of a full-length mirror and danced in front of her reflection. "I am so beautiful," she murmured to herself.

The confidence of her whirling poses and self-compliment struck me. Here was a child who I thought should be shriveling in self-pity. Instead she was twirling around, having fun. I felt humbled by her inner strength and honored to witness her joy in just being alive. I reached out and embraced her. "Yes, Sarah, you are beautiful."

Michele Wallace Campanelli

Promises to Keep

Knowledge is learning something every day. Wisdom is letting go of something every day.

ZEN SAYING

I'm a teacher. But there are days, like today, when I wonder why. It's been a tough day. The results of an English quiz taken by my fifth-graders were dismal. Despite my best efforts, the world of pronouns remains a mystery to them. How I wish there is a way to make the study of our language as exciting as a computer game, so the glazed looks would not appear in their eyes at the mention of the word "grammar."

I wanted to spend my lunch period thinking of a way to enrich the next day's lesson, but a child became sick and needed me to gather her assignments while she waited for her mother. It took longer than I thought so there wasn't time for lunch. Then an argument broke out at recess. Angry boys needed to be calmed and hurt feelings soothed before we could return to the classroom. We were all emotionally spent and found it hard to return to history books and Revolutionary War battles.

Hunger had given me a nagging headache, lingering long after the last child filed out for car pool. Now, hours later as I drive home, rubbing aching temples, I remember my husband's words, delivered like a lecture, after other days like this. "Why don't you quit? You'd probably make more money doing something else, and you wouldn't have papers to grade every night."

This late afternoon, I'm considering the wisdom of his words. I have a stack of papers to grade, which I promised my fifth-graders I would return tomorrow. But tonight a friend, whom I haven't seen in a year, is visiting from Belgium, and I told her I would keep this evening free.

Frustration builds as traffic slows, and I realize it's rush hour. No matter how hard I try, I can't seem to get out of my classroom ahead of the traffic. The world of my profession, a world filled with children, requires so much time. After school today, we had a faculty meeting. Events had to be planned, problems solved, new ideas discussed. So many details to remember. Just when I thought my day was over, a student peeked her head into the classroom to remind me I had promised to help her with a difficult assignment. The building was empty when I returned her to her waiting mother and wearily walked to my car.

Sitting in traffic threaded behind a distant stoplight, it's hard not to replay the day and revisit the tension. I turn up the air conditioner, hoping the coolness will ease my frustration and aching head. The last notes of a familiar melody are interrupted by news from the real world. Stock prices are down. Crime is up. The sound of gunfire fills the car as a broadcaster reveals the horror of life in a distant country. A strained voice reports the body of a local youngster, missing for weeks, has been identified. Click. Too much real world has invaded my space.

This missing child has had a profound effect on my fifth-graders. Every morning since she was first reported missing, my children have discussed news reports about her and prayed for her safe return.

Their concern was not only for her and her family but also for themselves. After all, she was one of them. A child believing herself to be safe and secure in her own neighborhood. My students, only one scant year younger than the tragic victim, wondered, "If it happened to her, could it happen to me?" Their thoughts and fears mirrored my own as I tried to find the right words to calm anxieties hoisted upon them by a world seemingly gone mad. There were no easy answers to quiet their apprehensions. How could I help them make sense out of senseless things and restore security to the small world of our classroom?

My children, ever wise with the innocence of youth, had found the answer themselves. They got out their pencils, markers and Crayolas and made cards. Cards written with words of compassion and love for a mother and father they didn't know. Cards that spoke of faith and the promise of peace. Cards adorned with ruby red hearts, golden crosses, spring flowers and rosy-cheeked angels. No grammar book, no lesson, could ever teach the beauty of the thoughts drawn and expressed by these children. Their cards, intended to comfort others, comforted the children themselves by leading them past the anxiety, back into the world of security that should be theirs.

As I sit in my car inching through the fumes of evening rush hour, I reflect on the strength of my students as they sought to right their world in the one way that made sense to them. I find myself smiling in spite of the heat, the traffic and the pile of ungraded tests. The rules of grammar might not have been learned today, but something bigger and better happened in my classroom. I just didn't recognize it at the time.

And then I remember. I remember why I'm still teaching. It's the children. They're more important than a lifetime filled with quiet evenings and more valuable than a pocket filled with money. The world of noise, pronouns, recess and homework is my world. My classroom, a child-filled world of discovery, of kindness and of caring is the real world. And I'm so lucky to be in it.

The traffic clears and I move past the stoplight, into the shady streets of my neighborhood. I'm glad to be home. It's time to call my friend and tell her I can't meet her tonight. I have promises to keep. She'll understand. After all, she's a teacher.

Kris Hamm Ross

Standing by Mr. Donato

*An education is not a thing one gets,
but a lifelong process.*

GLORIA STEINEM

If an important measure of success is
how much people respect and think of
you, if it's the lengths they will go to stand
firmly in your corner and never budge an
inch from your side, then Richard Donato
is one of the most successful men in the
San Fernando Valley today.

No one at Calahan Street Elementary
School would let this thirty-eight-year-old

custodian go without a fight. When they learned he would lose his job as plant manager unless he passed a high school equivalency test, everyone from the principal's office to the cafeteria workers got involved. Mr. Donato had to score an eighty-one on the test, but on his first try, the best he could muster was a weak forty-one. This high school dropout from New York, who had made such an impact on this school with his hard work, humor and sage advice to kids, was about to be cut loose. The road uphill was steep, and time was short.

Calahan Street Elementary rolled up its sleeves and got to work. Teachers came in early and stayed late, tutoring Mr. Donato on their own time. Kids stopped him in the hallways and told him to hang in there. "Study hard Mr. Donato, just like you always tell us to do."

Mr. Donato gave up his lunch and recess breaks to study with teachers Mandy

Price, Linda Babb and others. Then he went to night school classes designed to help him pass the test.

The results began to show.

The forty-one score moved up to a fifty on his next try. The fifty became a sixty-four on the test after that. And the sixty-four became a seventy-six.

Five points. So close. But the clock had just about run out. Word spread throughout school that if Mr. Donato didn't pass the test this Saturday, he was gone from Calahan—transferred to another school and a custodial job that didn't require a high school diploma.

Calahan Street went into a full-court press.

Kids got out their crayons and wrote letters to anyone with any clout in the school district, telling them how much Mr. Donato meant to them, how they loved him, and please, let him stay.

Teachers and office workers wrote

letters of their own, detailing how Mr. Donato was the first to arrive in the morning and the last to leave at night; how there wasn't a speck of graffiti on this campus, and every classroom was swept clean every morning.

The school custodian may have no high school diploma, they wrote, *but that doesn't mean he isn't one of the sharpest, wisest employees on this campus.*

We aren't asking that Rich be excused from the test, only that he be allowed to stay at Calahan until he passes, Mandy Price wrote. *We all know he can do it.*

But, as educators, they also knew the flip side of their efforts. They knew the anxiety that comes to anyone, from CEOs to custodians, when success is so close. Would Mr. Donato's score continue to rise, or would the pressure be so great that his grade would drop, depriving him of those precious five points he desperately needed to keep his job?

On Friday, the day before the test, the telephone in Principal Rick Wetzell's office rang. There had been a miscommunication, he was told. Because Mr. Donato had been with the school district for ten years, he was "grandfathered" in. Only new hires needed to have a high school diploma.

Mr. Donato's job was safe.

By midday Friday, the entire school knew Rich would be staying. He didn't need to pass the test anymore.

"Yes, I do," Richard Donato said respectfully. "I have to pass it for my wife and three young children. I have to pass it for myself."

It's like he always told the troubled kids who teachers brought to him for a little talking to. Kids headed down the same wrong road he had taken growing up in New York City. "You gotta stay in school and you gotta try," Donato would say. "The other way is the loser's way."

Now, the sage custodian had a chance to

show all the kids at Calahan with action, not words.

Mandy Price answered her phone at home Saturday at noon.

"Is this Mrs. Price, the woman who helped me *pass this test?*"

Too choked up to respond, Mandy could only smile and cheer inside for everyone at Calahan Street Elementary School. Richard Donato scored an eighty-one.

Dennis McCarthy

One of My Early Teaching Jobs

The object of teaching a child is to enable him to get along without his teacher.

ELBERT HUBBARD

One of my early teaching jobs involved teaching at an alternative school. This school had "the worst of the worst," the students that even public alternative schools had expelled. The students who straggled in the door every day were living lives of quiet desperation, labeled as failures and never expected to amount to anything. Our school had an on-premise day care, so we had a lot of teen mothers who were trying to break free of their cycle of poverty. Every student who came to us realized we were the last chance they had to make something of their lives.

As a fairly new teacher, I was terrified of them. They were mostly African-Americans from the inner-city, and I was a white teacher who grew up in the affluent suburbs. I had visions of what they were like gleaned from countless hours of television and movies. I was sure these kids were violent, amoral people, and somehow I envisioned myself as their savior, the person who would turn their lives from violence and poverty to peace and prosperity. I couldn't have been more wrong.

My first day there, the students knew they had me in a corner and took advantage of every misstep I made. The first scene in *Dangerous Minds* could have been my classroom, and I had no ex-Marine moves to get their attention. I was scared and nervous, and I wondered why I ever thought I could teach these incorrigibles. As I was about to leave, certain that I would turn in my resignation that afternoon, one of my students came over and said, "Oh, you'll be okay. They's just testin' you." With a smile, he sauntered out.

I have never been a person to turn down a challenge, so I came back the next day and the next and the day after that. After a while, the challenges came less often, and I knew I had "made it" when I heard one of our students tell another, "You got Miz Nelson? Yeah, she cool."

I came to the school determined to teach the students how to read. Instead, the students taught me how to live. I learned what it is like to be truly poor, to be told that you are nothing and to have suspicion and fear follow you every day of your life. I learned about the joy you can find in the little things in life and why teenagers want to have babies. I learned what makes a young man join a gang and even take a life. When the student who had reassured me that first day was cut down in a drive-by shooting, I learned a lot about grief. I learned even more about the human spirit and how truly resilient it could be.

My homeroom students were the most special to me. I saw them every morning when we prepared for the rest of their day. We talked about what was going on at home, at school, and everything and anything they wanted or needed to discuss. In the afternoon, before they left, we had study hall and again talked about what was going on in their lives.

Each homeroom teacher was responsible for his or her homeroom kids. We were their advocates, their friends and, for some, very much their "parents" since many of these kids didn't have an available parent figure. If they didn't come to school, we found out why. We visited their homes to meet their families, and we were available at every turn at school to give whatever assistance was needed.

Then, midway through the year the announcement came. The organization that had sponsored us had sold the land, and at the end of the year, our school would be closed.

We teachers were devastated. We loved our kids like our own, and we hated to let them go. The students were even more destroyed. This school was their last chance. Many of them literally had nowhere to go. The public schools had expelled them, and no one else would take them either. Once again, they would fail.

The students responded to the news with one of two attitudes. Many just dropped out, feeling rejected again. Those who stayed decided to work until their last breath and get as much as they could from school. When protest after protest failed, they finally resigned themselves to the fact that they would be moving on. They chose new schools or stepped up their work so they could graduate with the final class.

As the school year came to a close, I wondered what I could give to these kids who had given me so much, who had taught me about myself, and about my prejudices, and about what is really important in life. I didn't have much money, and I knew that material gifts wouldn't impress many of them anyway. So I wrote each student a letter telling them about the wonderful qualities I saw in them, my hopes and dreams for their futures, and the ways they had changed my life. I told each of them that I loved them.

The day before the last day, I handed out the letters and waited calmly, expecting these "tough" kids to reject my words and toss them into the trash. Instead, I was met with absolute silence.

"Do you really mean this?" one asked.

"Of course. Every word."

"Wow."

One big hulking boy, who had never succeeded in school until he came to us, sat silently in a corner of the room. I thought he was just waiting for the moment I wasn't looking so he could throw my letter out. Instead, he came over, hugged me and sobbed. I heard him say, "No one ever told me that I was this good before."

My heart broke. Imagine living your life for eighteen years and never having anyone tell you how valuable and special you are, to not be recognized for being important in the world. I couldn't fathom the despair with which this child had lived his life.

That day, I determined that my role as a reading teacher was not merely to teach students to read, but much more importantly, to teach them of their value in life. To this day, every holiday, I write every one of my students a letter telling them about the gift they are to me and their classmates. It never fails that a few kids cry, and most of them are amazed that someone cared enough to tell them they are valuable people. The letters are tucked quietly into notebooks and some even stapled into binders, lest the letter be lost and the reminder of their value be gone forever.

I often think of those kids and wonder if they know how many lives they have truly touched by having first touched mine.

Angela K. Nelson

So Little Meant So Much

My plan was to slip out of the conference before the keynote speech to avoid rushing to the airport. The wind-up luncheon featured Sandra McBrayer, the 1994 National Teacher. I can't remember why I remained seated while she took her place at the podium, but I will never forget the story she told.

Sandra discarded her prepared speech and talked straight from her heart. She told us about a bright, enthusiastic young man she had taught in high school. He was constantly frightened and was the target of repeated severe beatings when several students learned he was gay. One day after school he went home, where he lived with his father, and told him what was happening at school. His father, mortified with his son's sexuality, replied with a beating even more brutal than any he had received at school and worse than others he had previously received from his father. At that point, he felt that the street was the only safe place left for him. Life there gave him his next dose of brutality as he was forced to earn sustenance money as a young prostitute.

One late night, after an especially abusive encounter, the young man's spirit was finally broken, and he felt he could not go on. He remembered one person who had showed him kindness. He reached out to his former teacher, Sandra McBrayer. She told him to stay by the pay phone and she would be there as soon as she could.

Within twenty minutes she found a slumped, quivering, bone-thin figure waiting for her, his hollow eyes swollen, but still holding a glimmer of trust and a trace of the smile she used to see. She told him to get in her car but wondered where she would take this young man. He had nowhere to sleep. Tonight, she knew that in order to survive, he needed much more than a homeless shelter could offer him. Going against "the rules," she decided to take him to her own house to give him warmth, something to eat, and mostly, some hope.

Sandra sat the frail, shaking young man in her kitchen and made soup. After hours of talking together, he seemed to calm down somewhat. He looked shyly at Sandra and surprised her with a request— a bath. Sandra got the bath ready, even adding bubbles, and then went back into the kitchen to clean up, wondering if perhaps she had overstepped her bounds as a teacher. Sure she had, she decided, yet she would do the same thing all over again, if necessary.

Suddenly, she heard sobbing that seemed to come from the depths of the young man's soul. When he came back into the kitchen a little later, Sandra gently asked him why he had been crying in the bathroom. The young man looked at her and said, "I'm sorry you heard me. I couldn't help it. I was so happy I couldn't stop crying. It was a dream I've had since I was a little boy. This was the first bath I ever had. I've always wanted to sit in a bathtub with bubbles."

I drove to the airport inspired to never give up encouraging other teachers. We may be the only people to ever have a positive influence on a child's life.

Beth Teolis

Permission to Fail

Experience is the name that everyone gives to his mistakes.

OSCAR WILDE

Each of us fails from time to time. If we are wise, we accept these failures as a necessary part of the learning process. But all too often as parents and teachers we deny this same right to our children. We convey either by words or by actions that failure is something to be ashamed of, that nothing but top performance meets with our approval.

When I see a child subject to this kind of pressure, I think of Donnie.

Donnie was my youngest third-grader. He was a shy, nervous perfectionist. His fear of failure kept him from classroom games that other children played with joyous abandon. He seldom answered questions—he might be wrong. Written assignments, especially math, reduced him to nail-biting frustration. He seldom finished his work because he repeatedly checked with me to be sure he hadn't made a mistake.

I tried my best to build his self-confidence. And I repeatedly asked God for direction. But nothing changed until midterm, when Mary Anne, a student teacher, was assigned to our classroom.

She was young and pretty, and she loved children. My pupils, Donnie included, adored her. But even enthusiastic, loving Mary Anne was baffled by this little boy who feared he might make a mistake.

Then one morning we were working math problems at the chalkboard. Donnie had copied the problems with painstaking neatness and filled in answers for the first row. Pleased with his progress, I left the children with Mary Anne and went for art materials. When I returned, Donnie was in tears. He'd missed the third problem.

My student teacher looked at me in despair. Suddenly her face brightened. From the desk we shared, she got a canister filled with pencils.

"Look, Donnie," she said, kneeling beside him and gently lifting the tear-stained face from his arms. "I've got something to show you." She removed the pencils, one at a time, and placed them on his desk.

"See these pencils, Donnie?" she continued. "They belong to Mrs. Lindstrom and me. See how the erasers are worn? That's because we make mistakes too. Lots of them. But we erase the mistakes and try again. That's what you must learn to do, too."

She kissed him and stood up. "Here," she said, "I'll leave one of these pencils on your desk so you'll remember that everybody makes mistakes, even teachers." Donnie looked up with love in his eyes and just a glimmer of a smile—the first I'd see on his face that year.

The pencil became Donnie's prized possession. That, together with Mary Anne's frequent encouragement and unfailing praise for even Donnie's small successes, gradually persuaded him that it's all right to make mistakes—as long as you erase them and try again.

Aletha Jane Lindstrom

What I Learned
in Spite of Myself

I was an air-force brat, which is a fine way to learn to adapt to new situations but a rotten way to get to know teachers. I never tried in school, because I always knew we'd be moving again, so why bother to please a teacher?

Then I met Mr. Fogarty.

My family moved for the last time, settling in Cannon Falls, Minnesota, where I finished high school. I was the class clown, but Mr. Fogarty had the nerve to see past my wisecracking surface to the intellect beneath. He had the nerve to expect me to—ugh—learn. Get good grades. Excel.

Naturally, I fought this. I'd been coasting just fine for years. I knew I wouldn't have trouble graduating. I wasn't planning to go to college, so who cared what my G.P.A. was?

I explained this to Mr. Fogarty during our student/teacher conference and left his classroom certain he understood what I required—namely, to be left alone to goof off until graduation.

The next day I discovered he had enrolled me in ISP.

ISP was an independent study program for the super-smart kids. I can't imagine the *strings* Mr. Fogarty must have pulled to get me, with my mediocre G.P.A. and smart-ass attitude, signed up. My jaw dropped when he explained that study hall—precious study hall, formerly used for napping!—would be devoted to working on independent study programs.

"*What* independent study programs?" I shrieked.

He remained unperturbed, although I was standing so close my yelling was blowing his bangs back from his forehead. "Whichever ones you like. Pick any two subjects you want to study."

I was furious at his interference. And a little flattered. Mr. Fogarty thought I was smart enough to be in a class with the likes of Marnie Ammentorp and Kirsten Hammer and Jessica Growette—the really smart kids. The last time a teacher took such an interest in my brain was to ask if I had suffered head trauma as a child, since I napped so much during school hours.

Outwardly, I remained irritated. *I'll fix him*, I thought. *Any two topics? Okey-dokey, pal. You asked for it.*

Mr. Fogarty was a religious man, a devoted father and easily embarrassed. I maliciously decided we would learn anatomy together. It would be torture for him; he'd drop this whole independent study nonsense, and I could go back to reading comics during study hall.

My plan didn't work. He got me a copy of *Gray's Anatomy* and we were off, starting with the names of the bones. All 206 of them. He didn't want to be there. I didn't want to be there. But he stuck it out and made me stick it out. While we studied metacarpals and metatarsals, he talked about the speech team.

As if it wasn't bad enough that I was memorizing the femur and the coccyx, now he was trying to sign me up for after-school activities. The man was insane!

He needed someone for the storytelling category. I resisted. He persisted. I told him I couldn't memorize a hundred stories in time for the tournament that weekend. He told me I could memorize a hundred thousand stories if I wanted. "You're not fooling anybody," he said. "I know there's a brain in there. Saturday, 8:00 a.m. Don't be late."

I wasn't late. I was amazed to find myself there, but I wasn't late. I was scared. I was sure I couldn't do the work, but Mr. Fogarty thought I could. And for the first time, I didn't want to disappoint my teacher.

Storytelling is just like it sounds . . . you read a big book of fairy tales (that year's book had 216 stories). Then you draw to find out what story you're supposed to tell. That's why it was important to read every story—if you drew one you hadn't read, you were sunk. You'd be standing in front of an audience and a judge with nothing to say.

I didn't have to worry about that; to my surprise, I'd easily read the stories in time. But I worried about the competition. The other storytellers were all tiny and had bows in their hair and big eyes and wore ruffled dresses. I towered over all my classmates and was darned near as tall as Mr. Fogarty. I was clumsy—always tripping or dropping things or stubbing my toe. I didn't wear bows; my hair was usually skinned back in a ponytail. The other storytellers all looked like Goldilocks; I looked like one of the bears.

"I can't do this," I whispered.

I was wasting my breath; Mr. Fogarty wasn't interested in hearing my protests at this stage. "You'll do great."

"No, I will *not*."

"Yes," he said cheerfully, giving me a shove toward the stage. "You will."

The key to successful storytelling is to really throw yourself into the story. So I ignored the audience and became Simple Simon, blundering about on the stage as Simon blundered about in his life. I couldn't believe the laughs I was getting.

Mr. Fogarty had been right again; out of fifty storytellers, I took second place. Team Goldilocks never knew what hit them.

After that I took first, second or third place at every tournament. By then I was fast friends with the smart kids; they had decided I was one of them.

Meanwhile, Mr. Fogarty and I were doggedly plowing through *Gray's Anatomy*. I now knew more about bones, cartilage and the nervous system than I ever wanted to know. And Mr. Fogarty told me I had to pick my second independent study program.

I groaned; would the madness never end? I'd accidentally gotten an A in biology thanks to my stupid independent study; I was fast losing my reputation as a slacker. And now I had to pick another topic?

I argued, but we both knew who was going to win this one—the same person who'd been winning all of them. So I picked writing, half expecting him to tell me I shouldn't, or couldn't.

He assigned me essays. He assigned me short stories. He made me read O'Henry,

Jackson, Bradbury, Chaucer. After I was saturated with words, he asked me to write. My first short story was about a little boy who kills his mother. I was incredibly proud of the gruesome thing and, although Mr. Fogarty was probably appalled, he encouraged me to send it in for publication. I confidently mailed it to *The New Yorker*.

Naturally, they sent me a rejection letter. I'm amazed they didn't set my story on fire and return the ashes. But Mr. Fogarty was as proud as if they'd printed my story on the cover. "A rejection from *The New Yorker*," he said admiringly, holding the letter as if it was spun gold. "That's really something. Most people will never see something like this." He put my rejection slip up on the bulletin board so everyone could see that I was (sort of) working with *The New Yorker*. Then he told me to write another story.

Mr. Fogarty was my speech coach and

teacher all through high school. He made me laugh; he made me furious; he made me try. Today, I've published six books, with four more coming out in the next two years. One of my books has gone into a second printing, and another won a national writing award, but because it was a sensual romance with some—ahem— explicit scenes, I never dared send it to Mr. Fogarty (making him study anatomy was bad enough). But he deserves a crate of books from me; he deserves a million crates. I owe him more than the books I wrote; he taught me to believe in myself, to have the confidence to dare what everyone else told me was impossible. It wasn't just that he expected me to try—he expected me to succeed. And once I started doing that, I found I had a taste for it. All because a teacher wouldn't give up on the smart-ass new kid.

Mr. Fogarty has touched my life in more ways than I could have dreamed, aside from helping me realize my dream of being published. I'm married to a Harvard graduate, a man from a wealthy family who was eating risotto when I was gulping down corn on the cob, the kind of man I once thought beyond my reach. And those smart kids on the speech team? The smart kids became the smart grown-ups and my dearest friends; our children play together.

Most amazing, I've been asked to teach at a writers' colony next summer. I'm nervous—I've never taught. But I'm going to do it anyway. For one thing, Mr. Fogarty would be appalled if he knew I was chickening out. For another, I've got the chance to touch the life of an aspiring writer, encourage her dream, help her be herself. Change her life forever.

Be a teacher.

MaryJanice Davidson

You Never Picked Me Last

*The direction in which education starts a
man will determine his future life.*

PLATO

"Dr. Carr! Is it you? Is it really you?"

I turned from where I had been browsing in the bookstore to see a six-foot-six-inch, muscular, good-looking, smiling, sandy-haired young man calling me. "It's me, Dr. Carr! Gibby!"

"Gibby, it can't be. You're all grown up!"

Looking closer, I would have known those eyes anywhere: serious, intense, penetrating blue eyes. Yes, it was my Gibby, all right.

He leaned down to hug his former elementary principal, and my thoughts went back to that shy, overweight little boy who transferred to our school as he began the fifth grade. He was quiet and withdrawn then.

Gibby had a difficult time the first few months, as do many children when they enter a new school. Some of the boys teased him about his lack of athletic ability when he attempted to play games on the playground. Gibby wasn't coordinated and had difficulty keeping up. He always appeared to be stumbling over his shoestrings. Most of the time, he was. I would remind him, "Better tie your shoestrings, Son," and he'd reply, "Yes, ma'am, Dr. Carr."

Often I would watch the students playing at recess. I noticed that when they began to choose up sides for a game, serious little Gibby would usually be left standing alone. Several times I went out on the playground and said, "I never get to

choose a team. May I?" The boys and girls
would laugh at their principal who wanted
to play and say, "Okay, Dr. Carr, it's your
turn!" I'd call out a few names and then,
around the fourth or fifth spot, I'd call
Gibby's name and a few others who never
seemed to get selected by their peers. My
team may not have been the best, but we
were, by far, the happiest and definitely
the most committed, determined and
loyal.

In the early spring of Gibby's fifth-grade
year, I held an exercise class on the playground during recess for anyone who
wanted to tone up their winter-weary
muscles. Girls flocked to this program, and
so did a few boys. Gibby was one of those.

We began by walking briskly around the
perimeter of the large playground. I led the
pack and Gibby invariably brought up the
rear, puffing and panting and tripping over
his shoestrings. As my group circled, we
would pass Gibby, who was giving it his

all, but nevertheless, lagging far behind. I'd call to him, "Good going, Gibby. Keep it up. You're getting the hang of it. Uh . . . better tie your shoestrings, Son."

"Yes, ma'am, Dr. Carr," he said, breathing hard and trying to put on a happy face.

After a month, Gibby shed a few pounds and didn't huff and puff as much. He still tripped over his shoestrings, but he did keep up with the group much easier.

By the fifth week, we had as many boys in our exercise class as girls. I don't believe the boys were suddenly all that interested in their health, for it was about this time the girls decided to dress in shorts. We added some floor exercises to our program and held this class in the gym. Gibby was right there, in the back row, stretching and bending, lifting and kicking, as intense as ever. Gibby never gave up or made excuses. The little fellow just wasn't a quitter. He tried harder than anyone, and I admired his spunk. Many of his classmates did, too. In time, he gained confidence and began to smile and talk more. He wasn't the new kid anymore, and he began to make some solid friends.

Now, after all those years, here we were standing in the bookstore. My little Gibby towered over me.

"What are you doing here, Gibby?" I asked. "I heard you had moved to Georgia."

"Yes, I live in Atlanta now, and I'm division manager of a computer software company. I'm visiting my mom here this weekend," he replied.

"Well, you look good and sound happy, Gibby."

"I am happy, and I think of you often. You know, it was kinda hard for me to change schools back then and move to a new town, but you were real nice to me."

"Why, thank you, Gibby."

"Yeah, you were always laughing, and you made it fun to come to school," he said. "I'll never forget your exercise classes. You really made us work."

Then a big smile lit up his face as he continued, "But, Dr. Carr, you know the thing that I remember most about you?"

"I have no idea. What was it?"

"Well," he said, as he stared at me with those deep blue eyes, "whenever you got a chance to choose up sides on the playground, you never picked me last."

"Of course not, Gibby. You were one of my most determined players."

We hugged again, and he said, "I'm married now. She's really nice and always laughing. Come to think of it, she's a lot like you. And the best thing about her is— from everyone in the world she could have married, she picked me. She picked me first!"

Tears flooded my eyes. I looked down to avoid his gaze and tried to regain my control.

It was then that I noticed his shoes.

"Better tie your shoestrings, "I mumbled,

wiping away my tears with the back of my hand.

"Yes, ma'am, Dr. Carr," he replied, flashing that boyish grin.

Tee Carr, Ed.D.

Anna

Benevolence alone will not make a teacher, nor will learning alone do it. The gift of teaching is a peculiar talent and implies a need and a craving in the teacher himself.

JOHN JAY CHAPMAN

Anna entered my life on a beautiful fall day in late August, behind her son, my new fifth-grader, William. Almost six feet tall, with striking green eyes, she had a freckled face framed in deep coppery hair. Reserved, as is the way with the northern New Mexico natives born in tiny mountainous towns, she introduced herself and her matching son with the musical Chicana accent. Both smiled shyly.

After a brief acquaintance period, I asked, "Would you like to help in the classroom? What helps the most is taking one day a month to grade a set of spelling and math papers."

"I wasn't so good in school," she almost whispered. "I only got to the eighth grade."

"Oh, that's okay," I said. "I'll help you."

She agreed, and I signed her up for the first Thursday of every month, beginning in September.

"Ms. Bucher?" Anna asked over the phone that first Thursday. "I don't know how to do this paper grading."

"I'll be right over," I stated.

I found her in her tiny, immaculate apartment, completely buried by the kids' work folders. Answer sheets were scattered everywhere. William was standing nervously over her back shoulder, obviously embarrassed that his mother couldn't help the teacher. It was clear that she was totally terrified at the task.

"You know, Anna," I began, "when I was in fifth grade, I didn't get math at all. My fear pulled the curtain down over the rest of my life for the next forty years. I thought that because I couldn't do multiplication right, or get the answers to story problems, I was dumb. It took teaching fifth grade, and having to learn my lessons each night, to cure my fear. "

They both smiled. Anna relaxed her hunched shoulders.

"Here is how you grade papers. . . ."

That began the first of many lessons with Anna. She was open, earnest and an intense listener. She breezed through paper grading and showed up at my classroom door after school asking if I needed help grading the "re-dos" in math. I almost kissed her! Anybody in our classroom who gets below a 75 percent must complete a "re-do," or sometimes "re-do-do-do." That means double, triple and quadruple paper grading to make sure the lesson is learned. Anna proved to be not only a dependable grader, but a tough one. She red-Xed every omitted decimal, dollar and operation sign, every word that was left out in a story problem, and marked those math papers with a vengeance and perfection. She calculated the appropriate grade mentally, never even needing the commercially bought sliding grader. Every kid knew that when Anna came, or the grading bag went home, they'd better mind their p's and q's, or suffer the low re-do grade.

Anna began to look more directly at the world, standing proud, speaking with her quiet reserve, but there was a determination, a purpose, stitching through her sentences.

In February of that year, I got a call.

"Mrs. Bucher," she began surely. "I want to help William with his colonial project. But I went to the library with him today, and I don't know how to get things."

The next day was Saturday, and we made a date to meet. I taught her how to use a card catalogue, the computer search, and showed her the numeric plan that catalogued the books. Finally, I introduced her to the information person at the desk.

"God sent you," Anna said with reverence and total belief. "Thank you, my teacher."

Starchy with purpose, she put her hand on William's shoulder and charged to the bookshelves. At about suppertime, I received another call.

"Ms. Bucher?" she began. "William and I went to three more libraries, and nobody knows anything about a silversmith named Paul Rivera."

I laughed so loud! It's one of those wonderful forever gifts that teachers get, linking them with a face, a willing heart, a kind spirit. She laughed, too, when I explained.

Of course she mastered the library system quickly, and William's completed diorama was a tiny cardboard hutch filled with pitchers, plates, silverware and candlesticks, fashioned from aluminum foil. And Paul Rivera was a period-dressed, hand-carved wooden figure, working at a table. William had carried on the traditions of his roots as the carver. Among the first settlers of New Mexico were deeply religious, master artisans who carved *Santos*, or saints. William's carving was beautiful, and so was his report and speech. He knew his silversmithing, and he added a bit about the northern New Mexico carvers of his family. Anna saw to that.

The last I heard, she was finishing her high-school education, with plans of becoming a fifth-grade teacher. Knowing Anna, she'll do it, and the world will have one more wonderful educator—who grades math with a vengeance.

Isabel Bearman Bucher

To Beth's First-Grade Teacher

*The secret of education
is respecting the pupil.*
RALPH WALDO EMERSON

I didn't know the man in front of me that morning. But I did notice that we both walked a little straighter, a little more proudly, as our daughters held our hands. We were proud but apprehensive on that important day. Our girls were beginning first grade. We were about to give them up, for a while at least, to the institution we call school. As we entered the building, he looked at me. Our eyes met just for a minute, but that was enough. Our love for our daughters, our hopes for their future, our concern for their well-being welled up in our eyes.

You, their teacher, met us at the door. You introduced yourself and showed the girls to their seats. We gave them each a good-bye kiss, and then we walked out the door. We didn't talk to each other on the way back to the parking lot and on to our respective jobs. We were too involved thinking about you.

There were so many things we wanted to tell you, Teacher. Too many things were left unsaid. So I'm writing to you. I'd like to tell you the things we didn't have time for that first morning.

I hope you noticed Beth's dress. She looked beautiful in it. Now I know you might think that's a father's prejudice, but she thinks she looks beautiful in it, and that's what's really important. Did you know we spent a full week searching the shopping malls for just the right dress for that special occasion? She wouldn't show you, but I'm sure she'd like you to know that she picked that dress because of the way it unfurled as she danced in front of the mirrors in the clothing store. The minute she tried it on, she knew she'd found her special dress. I wonder if you noticed. Just a word from you would make that dress all the more wondrous.

Her shoes tell you a lot about Beth and a lot about her family. At least they're worth a minute of your time. Yes, they're blue shoes with one strap. Solid, well-made shoes, not too stylish, you know the kind. What you don't know is how we argued about getting the kind of shoes she said all the girls would be wearing. We said no to plastic shoes in purple or pink or orange.

Beth was worried that the other kids

would laugh at her baby shoes. In the end she tried the solid blue ones on and, with a smile, told us she always did like strap shoes. That's the first-born, eager to please. She's like the shoes—solid and reliable. How she'd love it if you mentioned those straps.

I hope you quickly notice that Beth is shy. She'll talk her head off when she gets to know you, but you'll have to make the first move. Don't mistake her quietness for lack of intelligence. Beth can read any children's book you put in front of her. She learned reading the way it should be taught. She learned it naturally, snuggled up in her bed with her mother and me reading her stories at naptime, at bedtime and at cuddling times throughout the day. To Beth, books are synonymous with good times and loving family. Please don't change her love of reading by making the learning of it a burdensome chore. It has taken us all her life to instill in her the joy of books and learning.

Did you know that Beth and her friends played school all summer in preparation for their first day? I should tell you about her class. Everybody in her class wrote something every day. She encouraged the other kids who said they couldn't think of anything to write about. She helped them with their spelling. She came to me upset one day. She said you might be disappointed in her because she didn't know how to spell "subtraction." She can do that now. If you would only ask her. Her play school this summer was filled with positive reinforcement and the quiet voice of a reassuring teacher. I hope that her fantasy world will be translated into reality in your classroom.

I know you're busy with all the things that a teacher does at the beginning of the school year, so I'll make this letter short.

But I did want you to know about the night before that first day. We got her lunch packed in the Care Bear lunch box. We got the backpack ready with the school supplies. We laid out her special dress and shoes, read a story, and then I shut off the lights. I gave her a kiss and started to walk out of the room. She called me back in and asked me if I knew that God wrote letters to people and put them in their minds.

I told her I never had heard that, but I asked if she had received a letter. She had. She said the letter told her that her first day of school was going to be one of the best days of her life. I wiped away a tear as I thought: *Please let it be so.*

Later that night I discovered a note Beth left me. It read, "I'm so lucky to have you for a dad." Well, Beth's first-grade teacher, I think you're so lucky to have her as a student. We're all counting on you. Every one of us who left our children and our dreams with you that day. As you take our youngsters by the hand, stand a little taller and walk a little prouder. Being a teacher carries with it an awesome responsibility.

Richard F. Abrahamson, Ph.D.
A 3rd Serving of Chicken Soup for the Soul

More Chicken Soup?

We enjoy hearing your reactions to the stories in *Chicken Soup for the Soul* books. Please let us know what your favorite stories were and how they affected you.

Many of the stories and poems you enjoy in *Chicken Soup for the Soul* books are submitted by readers like you who had read earlier *Chicken Soup for the Soul* selections.

We invite you to contribute a story to one of these future volumes.

Stories may be up to 1,200 words and

must uplift or inspire. To obtain a copy of our submission guidelines and a listing of upcoming Chicken Soup books, please write, fax or check our Web sites.

Chicken Soup for the Soul
P.O. Box 30880
Santa Barbara, CA 93130
Fax: 805-563-2945
Web sites: *www.chickensoup.com*

Supporting Teachers Around the World

In the spirit of supporting teachers around the world in becoming more effective teachers, a portion of the proceeds from the original *Chicken Soup for the Teacher's Soul* are donated to the International Council for Self-Esteem.

The Council is a nonprofit organization composed of representatives from over sixty countries networking together to share research, expertise, information and resources related to self-esteem. Their purpose is to promote public and personal awareness of the benefits of a healthy sense of self-esteem and personal responsibility, and to establish conditions within families, schools, businesses and governments that foster these qualities. One of its most important functions is to sponsor conferences and trainings on self-esteem for educators. These have been held in the United States, Norway, Greece, Argentina, Slovenia and Malaysia.

If you would like more information on the Council, their activities, services, resources and future conferences, you can contact them at:

International Council for Self-Esteem
234 Montgomery Lane
Port Ludlow, WA 98365
E-mail: *Esteem1@aol.com*
Web site: *www.self-esteem-international.org*

Who Is Jack Canfield?

Jack Canfield is one of America's leading experts in the development of human potential and personal effectiveness. He is both a dynamic, entertaining speaker and a highly sought-after trainer. Jack has a wonderful ability to inform and inspire audiences toward increased levels of self-esteem and peak performance.

In addition to the *Chicken Soup for the Soul* series, Jack has coauthored numerous books, including his most recent release, *The Success Principles, How to Get From Where*

You Are to Where You Want to Be with Janet Switzer, *The Aladdin Factor* with Mark Victor Hansen, *100 Ways to Build Self-Concept in the Classroom* with Harold C. Wells, *Heart at Work* with Jacqueline Miller and *The Power of Focus* with Les Hewitt and Mark Victor Hansen.

Jack is regularly seen on television shows such as *Good Morning America, 20/20* and *NBC Nightly News.* For further information about Jack's books, tapes and training programs, or to schedule him for a presentation, please contact:

Self-Esteem Seminars
P.O. Box 30880
Santa Barbara, CA 93130
Phone: 805-563-2935 • Fax: 805-563-2945
Web site: *www.chickensoup.com*

Who Is Mark Victor Hansen?

In the area of human potential, no one is better known and more respected than Mark Victor Hansen. For more than thirty years, Mark has focused solely on helping people from all walks of life reshape their personal vision of what's possible.

He is a sought-after keynote speaker, bestselling author and marketing maven. Mark is a prolific writer with many best-selling books such as *The One Minute Millionaire, The Power of Focus, The Aladdin Factor* and *Dare to Win,* in addition to the

Chicken Soup for the Soul series.

Mark has appeared on *Oprah, CNN* and *The Today Show,* and has been featured in *Time, U.S. News & World Report, USA Today, New York Times* and *Entrepreneur* and countless radio and newspaper interviews.

As a passionate philanthropist and humanitarian, he has been the recipient of numerous awards that honor his entrepreneurial spirit, philanthropic heart and business acumen for his extraordinary life achievements, which stand as a powerful example that the free enterprise system still offers opportunity to all.

Mark Victor Hansen & Associates, Inc.
P.O. Box 7665
Newport Beach, CA 92658
Phone: 949-764-2640 • Fax: 949-722-6912
Web site: *www.markvictorhansen.com*

Contributors

If you would like to contact any of the contributors for information about their writing or would like to invite them to speak in your community, look for their contact information included in their biography.

Richard F. Abrahamson, Ph.D., is a Professor of Literature for Children and Adolescents in the College of Education at the University of Houston. An author of more than 150 publications on children's books and reading motivation, Abrahamson is the winner of the Education Press Association Award for Excellence in Educational Journalism. He is a frequent consultant to school districts and keynote speaker at conferences dealing with juvenile literature and reading motivation. He can be reached at the University of Houston, Department of Curriculum & Instruction, 256 Farish Hall, Houston, TX 77204-5027.

Bonnie Block currently trains and consults for childcare providers in Baltimore County Public Schools and at state and national levels. She was Teacher of the Year for Baltimore County and a finalist for the State of Maryland. Bonnie has a passionate commitment to helping individuals achieve success. Reach her at *bbhugs@earth link.net.*

Isabel Bearman Bucher retired from teaching and is having a neverending honeymoon with life. This is her second story for *Chicken Soup for the Soul.* Her first story, "The Melding," appeared in *A Second Chicken Soup for the Woman's Soul.* She has completed a 70,000-word memoir entitled *Nonno's Monkey, An Italian American Memoir,* and continues to write stories of the heart. Many of her students keep her in their lives when they marry, have babies and need help on college exams. She and her husband, Robert, travel, dividing their time between their Taos, New Mexico, Ski Valley cabin and the world doing home exchanges. Isabel's eldest daughter, now a teacher, asks her mother to mentor her, which is a joy and an honor.

Michele Wallace Campanelli is a two-time national bestselling author. She was born on the Space Coast of Florida where she resides with her husband, Louis, and pet iguana, Jamison. Michele welcomes fans to e-mail her with comments at *www.michelecampanelli.com.*

Tee Carr, Ed.D., is the author of three books for teachers: *All Eyes Up Here! A Portrait of Effective Teaching, How Come the Wise Men Are in the Dempster Dumpster?* and *School Bells and Inkwells: Favorite School Stories and More!* Tee enjoyed over twenty years as a teacher, principal and university supervisor of student teachers. She and her husband, Jack, both educators, reside in Chattanooga, Tennessee. To order books or reach the author, contact Carr Enterprises, 3 Belvoir Circle, Chattanooga, TN 37412. Call 423-698-5685. E-mail: *drtcarr@aol.com* or fax: 423-698-3182.

MaryJanice Davidson has written several critically acclaimed novels and won the Sapphire Award for Best Science Fiction Romance. Her first book, *Adventures of the Teen Furies*, recently made the young adult bestseller list. She lives in Minnesota with her husband and children, and occasionally runs into Mr. Fogarty. For more information on MaryJanice's books, visit her Web site at *www.maryjanicedavidson.com.*

Dennis McCarthy has been a *Los Angeles Daily News* columnist since 1984. He has won numerous journalism awards in his career, including being named "Best Columnist in California" twice by the California Newspaper Publishers Association and "Journalist of the Year" by the Los Angeles Press Club. McCarthy's four-day-a-week column stresses the poignant, human-interest stories of the average working people who step out of the shadows to do something that makes their community better and safer for everyone. He is married with four children, one still living at home drawing a modest allowance.

Angela K. Nelson received her Masters of Science in Reading in 1998 from the University of Nebraska at Omaha. She is a remedial reading specialist/mentoring program coordinator for Westside Schools. Angela has devoted her career to at-risk youth. She is an accomplished public speaker and can be reached at *anelson@westside66.org*.

Kay Conner Pliszka was a teacher for twenty-eight years. Her extensive work with at-risk teens brought school and community awards from Wisconsin Bell/Ameritech, MCADD, Walkers Point, State Exemplary Educational Grants, and an inclusion in *Who's Who Among American Teachers*. Now a motivational speaker, Kay shares her humorous, turbulent and inspirational experiences from teaching. Write to her at 1294 Weaton Ct., The Villages, FL 32162 or *K.PLISZKA@prodigy.net.*

Kris Hamm Ross lives in Houston, Texas, and has devoted the past fifteen years as a teacher to helping children discover the power and beauty of the written word. She is a published writer whose favorite subjects include education and the people and everyday events that touch her life. Please e-mail her at *klross@pdq.net.*

Beth Teolis, M.Ed., enjoys living her passion of enabling educators to appreciate how significant they can be influencing the lives of their students. Inspired after attending three of Jack Canfield's Self-Esteem Facilitating Seminars, she has authored books and presented workshops for educators and parents so that they may be aware just how important their roles are. Beth is the author of *Ready-to-Use Self-Esteem & Conflict Solving Activities for Grades 4–8* and *Ready-to-Use Conflict Resolution Activities for Elementary Students,* both published by Pearson

Education. To order by phone in the U.S.: 800-288-4745; in Canada: 800-361-6128; and for international orders: 201-767-4900. Beth is president of Life Skills Associates International, a member of the National Speakers' Association, founder of the Canadian Council for Self-Esteem, and a member of the executive board of the International Council for Self-Esteem. Beth is now on a task force to initiate ParentCoaching at the Adler Professional Schools so that it will reach all parents. Contact Beth at *teolis@msn.com*.

Carol Toussie Weingarten received her Bachelor of Arts from Barnard College of Columbia University, Master of Science in Nursing from New York Medical College, and Master of Arts and Doctor of Philosophy degrees in Nursing from New York University. An author, educator, speaker and practicing nurse, she is an associate professor at Villanova University. E-mail her at *carol.weingarten@ villanova.edu.*